The Song in the Thread - Saint Thérèse of Lisieux
Text by Bronwyn Finch
Illustrations by Mark Anderson

ISBN: 978-1-989647-74-5
First published September 25, 2025
Toronto, Canada

Text copyright © 2025 Bronwyn Finch
Illustrations copyright © 2025 Mark Anderson

All rights reserved. No part of this book may be reproduced, stored in a retrieval system, or transmitted in any form or by any means—electronic, mechanical, photocopying, recording, or otherwise—without the prior written permission of the publisher, except in the case of brief quotations embodied in critical articles or reviews.

This is a work of creative storytelling inspired by the life of The Song in the Thread - Saint Thérèse of Lisieux (1873–1897). It is not a historical or theological text. Any resemblance to specific persons, living or deceased, outside of its historical inspiration, is purely coincidental.

Publisher: The Evergreen Centre
Publisher's Cataloging-in-Publication Data

Finch, Bronwyn.
    The Song in the Thread - Saint Thérèse of Lisieux / text by Bronwyn Finch ; illustrations by Mark Anderson. — First edition.
    Summary: A gentle tale inspired by Saint Thérèse of Lisieux, who believed that even the smallest tasks, done with great love, could be a way to show devotion to God.
    Identifiers: ISBN 978-1-989647-74-5
    Subjects: Saint Thérèse of Lisieux 1873-1897—Juvenile literature. | Monks—Juvenile literature. | Mindfulness—Juvenile literature. | Christian life—Juvenile literature.
    Classification: 248.4—dc23

The Song in the Thread
Saint Thérèse of Lisieux

by Bronwyn Finch

In a town of soft, rolling hills,
Thérèse watched the garden bloom.
Church bells chimed overhead.
A quiet joy hummed beneath the day.
She felt it there, in the little things.

Her hands were small, her body frail,
but her heart stretched wide,
like sunlight spilling over hills.
Every breath, every glance—
a secret song of love.

Hugs became prayers.
Smiles became soft gifts.
She didn't need words;
love whispered from their eyes:
"I am here."

Her heart found its home in a cloister.
Stone walls. Wooden doors.
A place of prayer. A place of quiet work.
They gave her a habit,
a cell,
and a needle and thread.

Marie became Sister Thérèse of the Child Jesus.
Not a scholar,
not a leader—
a helper with her hands.
Needles danced. Threads flowed.
In the small, she sang to God.

She sewed altar cloths,
stitch by tiny stitch.
Each thread a devotion.
"This I offer to You,"
she whispered to God.

Others saw simple sewing.
She saw grace.
Tiny knots held love.
Fine linen warmed her touch.
Even the snip of scissors sang.

"I sew with love," she thought,
"and when the task is done,
I offer it with joy."
In the small, she sang to God.

The sisters began to notice.
"Why is Sister Thérèse so peaceful?"
"Why does the workroom feel so filled with grace?"
They came not for cloth—
but for her heart.

"No need for grand gestures," she said.
"Sew, write, pray—
let your small acts sing.
God is here,
    in every little thing."

Outside of the convent,
Sister Thérèse's words, simple and true,
spread like petals.
People read and felt hope:
God was near—
in threads, in ink, in every breath.

When Sister Thérèse grew weak,
her hands slowed,
but, her love never faded.
She sewed with care.
She smiled with her whole heart.

When she was gone,
the workroom felt still.
But only for a moment.
The quiet remained—
like a gentle song in the world.

And today,
if you sew a seam slowly,
or write a kind word with love,
or sit in quiet thought—
you might feel it too.

A warmth.
A whisper.
A presence.

"I am here," you say.
"And You are too."
In the small, you find God.
Just like Sister Thérèse.

Saint Thérèse of Lisieux (1873–1897) was a young French Carmelite nun who lived in a monastery in Lisieux, France. Born Marie Françoise-Thérèse Martin, she grew up in a loving family and felt a deep connection to God from a young age.

Despite facing illness and entering the strict Carmelite order at just fifteen, Thérèse found joy and purpose in the simple acts of daily life within the monastery walls.

Saint Thérèse believed that even the smallest tasks, done with great love, could be a way to show devotion to God. Whether sewing vestments for the priests or writing letters to her family and spiritual sisters, she poured her heart into each action.

Her **"Little Way"** of spirituality emphasized humility, trust in God's love, and finding the extraordinary in the ordinary.

Her writings, especially her autobiography **Story of a Soul**, have inspired countless people with their simple yet profound message of love and faith.

The Little Way: Finding God in Small Things Practicing Love in the Ordinary

Saint Thérèse of Lisieux showed us that we do not need grand deeds to love God.

Even the tiniest moments—quiet work, gentle words, small sacrifices—can become prayers.

This is her **"Little Way"** of love.

Writing a Letter
A pen scratches the page.
Words carry love.
Even simple words, written with a kind heart, can make someone smile.
God, help my words be a gift to others.

Sewing a Stitch
Tiny threads twist and turn.
Each stitch holds care.
Every little knot adds to something beautiful.
God, help me be faithful in the smallest tasks.

Making a Bed
Sheets are straightened, pillows fluffed.
A quiet act of order and care.
Even a small tidy space can be a gift.
God, I offer this work to You with love.

Reading a Book
Pages turn softly.
Stories whisper kindness and truth.
Listening with our hearts teaches us more than words.
God, open my heart to what You want to teach me.

Tidying a Room
Hands place things gently in their spots.
No applause, no thanks—just love.
Even unseen care makes a difference.
God, help me do unseen things with a cheerful heart.

Picking a Flower
A single bloom in a small hand.
Beauty offered with love can brighten the day.
God, help me share the small gifts You give me.

Staying Quiet
The world hums softly around you.
Listening is an act of love.
Sometimes, being still is the kindest thing we can do.
God, help me wait on You with a peaceful heart.

Helping a Sister
Hands reach out to help.
Even when tired, care matters.
A gentle touch can be a prayer in action.
God, help me serve others with joy.

Lighting a Candle
A tiny flame flickers.
Light pushes back darkness.
Even a little spark can shine far.
God, let my life be a small light for others.

Waking Up with Joy
Morning stretches, soft and new.
A fresh day, a fresh heart, a fresh chance.
Smile at the sun. Step into love.
God, help me greet this day with gratitude.

Closing Blessing
May your small acts bloom with love.
May you find God in quiet moments, gentle words, and everyday tasks.
God is here—in writing, in sewing, in helping, and in waiting. attentive,
  and your work a prayer.

www.ingramcontent.com/pod-product-compliance
Lightning Source LLC
Chambersburg PA
CBHW061356010526
44107CB00012B/953